when word and image run away
the selected poems of Mary Blinn

Editors:
Albert DeGenova
P. Hertel

After Hours Press
Elmwood Park, Illinois
2016

Table of Contents

All artwork by Mary Blinn

Foreword
    Albert DeGenova 7
Remembering Mary Blinn
    The Editors 9

Poems 1993 - 1999
    Silver Spikes 13
    Testament 14
    His Treasure 16
    Snapshot 17
    The Dreamer 18
    Cinderella Story 19
    The Nature of Art 20
    American Rocket 21
    An Understanding 22
    On The Ferlinghetti Plane 23
    Apples in October 25
    The Woman Who Couldn't Leave The House 26

Poems 2000 - 2005
    Age of Reason 31
    Love Poem 32
    Morning Moon 33
    Waiting for The Children to Come 35
    Married Love 37
    Short Visit (to Uncle) 38
    Uncommon Ritual 40
    Conversation in Color 44
    People on The Street Exploding 45
    Gold and Purple 47

I See Faces 49
Morning on Cape Cod 50
The Kennedys Are Dead 51
Waking 53

Poems 2006 - 2014

Garden in Autumn 57
Patterns 59
Gas 60
Walking into Glass 61
Player Dog 63
Cigarette Break 64
Joyride 65
Private Ceremony 67
Sad As Juliet 68
Higher Ground 69
Winter Sky 70
Spring Rain (Poetry Month) 71
Late Bloomer 73

When Words and Image Run Away
The Selected Poems of Mary Blinn
ISBN 978-0-692-72415-6
Copyright © 2016 After Hours Press
www.afterhourspress.com

Albert DeGenova

Foreword

As is our tradition, *After Hours* magazine held a contributors' reading in August of 2015, celebrating the release of Summer Issue #31. Quraysh Ali Lansana was the featured writer in that issue, and was also the featured reader at the event. This contributors' reading, however, was a little different, because it also celebrated the poetry of *After Hours* regular contributor, featured writer (Issue #17), and friend Mary Blinn. Mary's sudden death just two months before had greatly saddened the Chicago poetry community.

That afternoon, several *After Hours* readers began their sets with one or two of Mary's poems. They brought to life Mary's voice, her poetic music, and her words. Quraysh (a poet, writer, teacher, editor, and one of *After Hours*' most distinguished featured writers) was immediately taken with Mary's poetry and made the strong suggestion that a collection of her poetry needed to exist, to make sure such a wonderful Chicago poetic voice would continue to be heard and read.

Thus began the spark that drove the creation of the book you hold in your hands. Through the careful cataloging of Mary's files, her husband Robert Blinn made the bulk of her work available to the editors. The result, *When Word and Image Run Away*, is a selection of Mary Blinn's finest poems, many of which were published in the pages of *After Hours*. Some of the illustrations, also by Mary, had appeared previously in *After Hours* as well.

After Hours Press has one mission and that is to promote the work of Chicago area (and Chicago-affiliated) writers and artists. Since June of 2000, the Press has created a showcase of Chicago writers and artists at the beginning of the 21st century. That platform has found a home at several universities, including the University of Chicago Library permanent archive. *When Word and Image Run Away, The Selected Poems of Mary Blinn* is the third book publication from After Hours Press. It is preceded by *The Professor's Quarters*, a collection of essays about teacher and Chicago writer Norbert Blei; and *Eating Brains*, a poetry chapbook by *After Hours* regular contributor Siegfried Mortkowitz.

The Editors

Remembering Mary Blinn

In 2015 the Chicago literary community was saddened by the loss of poet and artist Mary Blinn.

Mary had been writing poetry for much of her life, but took up the craft in earnest in the 1990s, winning a prize with one of her earliest efforts, "His Treasure," in 1993. More than a poet, however, Mary was also a singer/songwriter and visual artist. Her CD of children's songs, "A Handful of Sunshine," which she wrote and performed, earned a Grammy nomination in 2002. She had numerous art exhibits and installations at galleries in and around Chicago, including a one-woman show at the Old Town Triangle gallery in 2013, and an open-air multimedia installation called "I See Faces" in Oak Park, IL.

Mary was highly regarded within the Chicago poetry scene. She was a regular contributor to the journal *After Hours* and frequently read her works at various area open mics and invitational readings, including the Printer's Row Literary Fest. She also received an Illinois State Poetry Award and a Pushcart Prize nomination. Mary got her master's degree in interdisciplinary arts from Columbia College, where she worked in the music department, and taught a freshman class in critical thinking.

In spite of all her accomplishments, Mary had remarkable humility and was always thrilled when a poem was published or she was asked to read. When she was suddenly faced with a devastating illness, her reaction was to start a project to make a multimedia book about her hospitalization – something to help other people who might share the same situation. Taking a bad experience and turning it into something creative to help other people is Quintessential Mary. Unfortunately, she wasn't able to complete that project; but in recognition of her talent and contributions to the poetry community, the editors of *After Hours* are pleased to bring you *The Selected Poems of Mary Blinn*.

Thank you, Mary, for all of the poetry you shared with us over the years. You will be greatly missed.

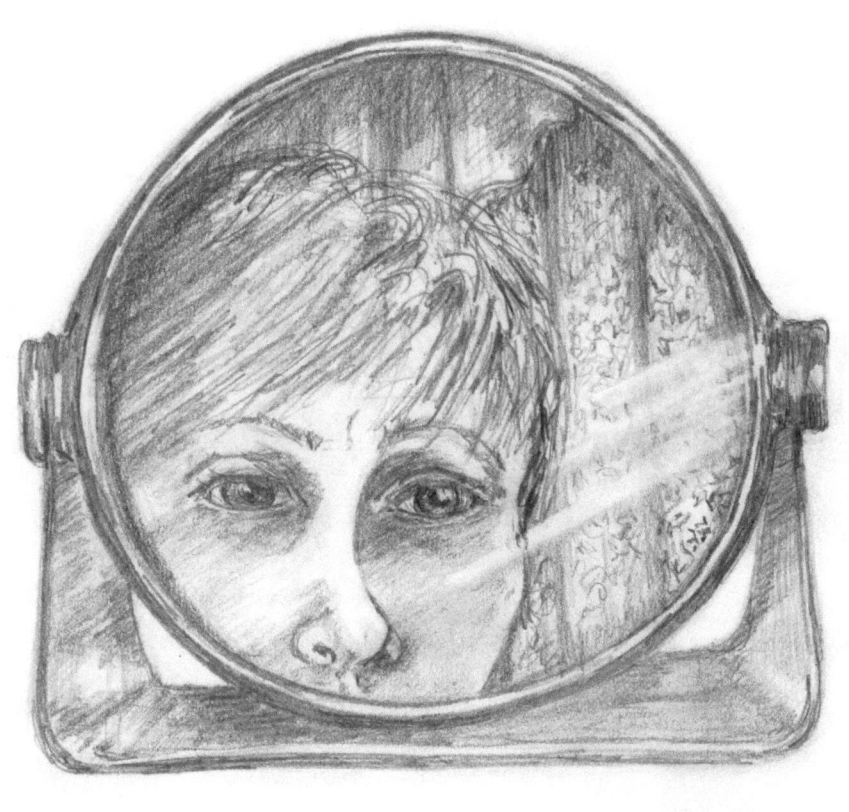

Self-Portrait 10-94

Poems 1993 - 1999

Silver Spikes

Flash in the dirt-streaked sunlight of
the second-hand shop window.
They glare at the passers-by
waiting to seduce some unsuspecting Dorothy into
clicking those magical heels home. Like a catfish
snagged by the glint of a lure in murky water,
I'm reeled in toward the

Hey babe what's doin' wanna little
razzle-dazzle hot jazz take me dancin' tonight
handsome pop the cork and watch it spray
kick 'em in the air and let fly until
the alka-seltzer sunrise lands us under the bed in
some downtown hotel what say kid
throw some tinsel on the old bones and
let's go live a little

Silver Spikes.

They look almost new; barely broken in.
A guaranteed blister on the skin.
Guess I was looking for a
more experienced pair.

Testament

The body of grief
lies still as death itself.
Shrouded in silence
and dark privacy;
wrapped in
layer upon layer of
denial, despair,
memory.
It waits with
interminable patience for
resurrection,
rejoicing.
With hesitant hand
trembling in the
presence of answered prayers,
I begin to unwind
the gauzy mystery
myself.

The child wakes and
turns his head
toward me.
He won't smile,
so I continue to
sing softly.
His newborn jewel

eyes sparkle with
an instant of
contentment he'll
never remember.
He drifts again into
heavenly peace,
and this moment
holds the truth:

there is nothing so sweet
as the lullaby sung
on the way up the road
to Golgotha.

His Treasure

Now they're both gone,
leaving a 38-year-old orphan
rifling like a thief in the closet,
tossing dust-covered shoes,
polyester sportcoats, and
age-stained dress shirts
into a carton marked
Salvation Army.
He never wore these things.
Empty hangers rock uselessly;
the tingling echoes
throughout the house.

Far back, against the wall,
my mother's bathrobe;
sleeves expertly folded flat
and crossed in the front,
neatly tucked into the belt
tied at the waist.
A patient pose,
created one lonesome evening
by his shaking hands, then left in peace.
removing his favorite flannel from the hook,
I place it, facing hers, on a hanger.
I tie them together, arm to arm.

Snapshot

We were better than sisters,
crouching head to head;
Kool-Aid grins
balanced on scabby knees.
A black and white glossy from
scalloped-edge days,
haunted by echoes of
whispered holiness.
We pressed our
blood-sticky wrists together
sealing the promise of friendship.

Windblown chestnut hair
surrounding a throaty giggle,
healed-over wounds on
adolescent limbs,
blurred the vow that
weakened without regret
until finally, there was
no pulse.
A grainy, grey photograph
taken an eternity ago
is all that remains.

She kept her darkest secret
three days; found
shattered on the carpet,
burn marks at the temple,
eyes frozen open
refusing the appearance of
peaceful sleep.
Lost somewhere in
her scrambled thoughts,
a memory, now crusted dry;
an endless summer's day.

The Dreamer

Asleep between humid sheets,
he breathes in slow,
satisfied rhythms.
A smile slips across the dreamer's face and
fingers twitch
momentarily;
grasp at inspirations that
flash like fireflies behind
the darkness of closed eyelids.
I cannot calculate the depth of deceptive serenity
that insulates this restless soul
lying next to me.
I lean over and lick the
salty sweat from his brow,
and having tasted,
thirst for more.

Cinderella Story

In the mirror sagging
adolescent flesh
crow's feet eyes, swollen
sinus bags tagged for
a distant landing.
I can't cover imperfection with
cheap cosmetics anymore and
the face you've come to
love is shoved in a make-up kit
rolled up in a pair of jeans that
sure don't fit like they used to.
The evil young step-sisters laugh
like macaques and click
their plastic cups of Perrier
while I dissolve to dust
and take flight.
Not so fancy.
Not tickled so easily as
some might like. Only
champagne can do that.
Well, pass the bottle and
fill my shoes,
these glass slippers are
bought and paid for.

The Nature of Art

There is an urgency to
the ant on a peony,
hairs for legs scrambling
round and round the bud
little hairy legs ripping
shredding round and round
some force greater than
its little ant self;
bulbous head rocking
rocking back and forth rocking
rocking back and rocking forth
scratching and scissor lips
tearing, gnawing to get at it
diligence
diligence
diligence
until there has to come one
final tear that makes the beauty
burst and we all go aaahhh
marvel at the miracle and bring
the flower to the dinner table.
Evicted ant down the drain
nothing left to cling to.

American Rocket

Once upon a time
one nickel, one dime
silver chimes
I scream we all scream
chase the white ice cream
truck in the heat
bare feet
sprint over griddle-hot concrete
and clothespin cards flapping in bicycle spokes
Bazooka Joe jokes
all the neighborhood kids coax
the truck to a stop
we want a popsicle
we want the red white and blue one
 we want the raspberry coconut cherry one
we want the shaped-like-a-spaceship one
we want
we want
we want the American Rocket
we empty our pockets
down to the patriotic lint
without flinching
it's our turn to lick
the American Dream on a stick
and stretching our lips too thin
to fit the whole thing in
we gain from our pain
a candy-flavored grin
stained on our satiated faces.

An Understanding

It's not much to ask, to be clean.
She swirls the rough institutional cloth
in the water, trying to soften the edges
so that it feels more like home to him.

She swirls the rough institutional cloth
until it's so hot it hurts,
so that it feels more like home to him.
Her knuckles turn red from twisting it dry

until it's so hot it hurts
and a droplet runs a path along her arm.
Her knuckles turn red from twisting it dry.
She presses the steaming cloth to his skin

and a droplet runs a path along her arm.
His eyes close as though he's already in heaven.
She presses the steaming cloth to his skin,
feeling the shudder of each desperate breath.

His eyes close as though he's already in heaven,
in the water, trying to soften the edges;
feeling the shudder of each desperate breath.
It's not much to ask, to be clean.

On The Ferlinghetti Plane

He comes to share his time
the wheelman who drove us into
here and now, and now
we're here – the furrow-browed poets,
discerning scholars, and aging
children of the beat generation.
All buckled in and
ready to ride that
Coney Island Express.
He takes the stage lanky legs,
ruddy cheeks, white hair generous
soul. Comes to share
not days gone but
gone days.
He releases the brake and
we ride his rhythm
breathe his breath
repeat his beat rise and dip.
His words tumble over the
lip of the stage and
we're caught in the headlights
after fifty odd years.
Big Daddy Driver is still
in control of the road.
He leaves us then
windblown, exhilarated,
ready to ride again.
The beat goes on, man.
The beat goes on.

Apples in October

Odd
how a mild breeze in autumn
can stir the dead;
carry fragments of conversation
whirl words around
your head like dry leaves
scraping along the pavement.
"Promise me," she said
leveling her most serious
concerned mother look,
"you'll never be so vain
you can't eat an apple when
you walk down the street."
I remember
I laughed.
October's breath flaps
my jacket like a sail
yet will not disturb
those swept neat, wordless
left for dead
at the edge of the curb.
Arms like wings spread
I take off running through the leaves
and kick every blessed one of them
into the air. Listen to
the wisdom rustle away.
I remember.
I laugh. And
I don't give a rat's ass if
anyone is watching.

The Woman Who Couldn't Leave The House

She must do it right
or not at all. Obey the order,
afraid more of imperfection
than its consequence. Check
the plug is pulled from the outlet again.
Check the off button on the remote control.

off. on. off. on. off. she cannot control
the voice that tells her do it right.
Did you do it right? Do it again.
Keep yourself safe, in order.
Straighten the border of the bedskirt. Check
the corners for imbalance, imperfection.

tug. tuck. tug. tuck. tug. Imperfection
all around where she dreams. where she has no control.
Where imbalance and harmony collide. Check
the corners. Do it right.
Did you do it right? In order
to be safe, do it again.

tug. tuck. tug. tuck. tug. check the plug again.
Cannot trust the imperfection
of even her own actions. Cannot order
the sun where to shine, or control
what it hides in the shadows. Did you do it right?
Or not at all? The lights – did you check

the lights? off. on. off. on. off. Check
the time. Running behind again.
Leave late or not at all. Can that clock be right?

She stands still and hears the imperfection
of her own breath – uneven, uneventful, out of control.
On the order

of madness. Keep yourself safe, in order.
In order to check that you are safe. In order to check
the borders. Check the corners. Control
the dreams. Did you do it right? Do it again.
And again. And each again leaves a layer of imperfection
and each layer of imperfection leads her right

back to the outlet. Did I do it right? Am I in order?
I won't allow imperfection. I'll check
the plug again. I am in control.

Poems 2000 - 2005

Age of Reason

Who made you?
God made me.
Da dada da dada dee
God made me a punkin-headed child
and the punkin-headed child
stood in the classroom
stood in the aisle all undecided
like a wasp just landed on her shoulder.

Who made you?
God made me.
dum dee dum dee dum dum dee
The sister could've told her to sit down.
The sister could've passed over the child.
Could've asked the giraffe-neck child
or the riff-raff child or any other child
that God had made.

Who made you?
God made me.
Doo da dum da doo dum dee
The punkin head stood for an hour in the aisle.
The sister carved her face with a jack-o-lantern smile,
scraped the child clean of original seeds,
lit a candle in the punkin head for everyone to see
how she reconciled God with the child He made.

Who made you?
God made me.
Die die die die die die dee
God made me a punkin-headed child.
A punkin-headed child with a jack-o-lantern smile.

Love Poem

I'm amazed at how thin
your skin is.
I see your soul
like a gift
wrapped in tissue,
anticipating,
as I loosen the ribbon
to undo
what separates
me from you.

Morning Moon

How many more mornings
will I see the moon float
whimsical with whiz-bang
white clouds in the early spring
sky, ask why it lingers
past its prime.
This morning
I want it to be mine
pluck it from the air
fix it on my ear
wear it as a pearl
like Audrey Hepburn
in *Breakfast at Tiffany's*
be delicate, chi-chi, free
everyone will tell me
You look splennndid dahling.
You look mahvelous dahling.
But I'm stuck in this ghastly traffic
without a foot-long cigarette holder
or a huge mushroom hat
and the morning moon fades so fast that
no one at the office will notice my earrings.
Quel dommage, dahling.
Quel dommage.

Waiting for The Children to Come

She sits on the carpeted landing
surrounded by sweet-featured porcelain
dollies in velvet dresses,
curly puppies and fuzzy bears and
floppy corduroy elves and santas
with little black boots. They
crowd the stairway almost up to
where the bedrooms are.
She's loved them,
the children of her friends,
from a distance;
watched them grow in
each Christmas card photograph;
waited for wonder to replace confusion;
waited for that blank baby look
to leave their faces.
She lifts one gift from the others,
odd-looking little thing
sewn striped-cloth clown,
only rounded stumps
for arms, stuffing stiff
from long storage.
This one was for Elizabeth,
but Elizabeth left her in the sixteenth week;
slipped quietly through her body
through her fingers
and she prayed that someone
smaller than a thumbnail
could not feel pain.
She buries the clown
back into the abundance of
gifts she wants to give,
and sits on the stair,
waiting for the children to come.

Married Love

Oh the creaks and groans
of this
old mattress serenading
us every night
under the weight
of married love
year after year
singing the praises of
you and me
dream and dream
our individual grooves
worn into one
warm comfortable valley
our bones click
I breathe your breath
you surround me with skin
I roll over
over over
in the folds of your soul
and sleep
beyond caring who
steals the blankets
tonight.

A Short Visit (to Uncle)

We enter in a flurry of flowers,
cakes and hugs, my husband,
sister and I, bearing no
resemblance to each other
or to him – pants hitched in the
back by suspenders, light summer shirt
scrunched up under his arms
just like dad
before he died
oblivious to discomfort.
Six months to three years.
We chatter, he weeps,
welcomes us with family bones
so weak now, and cancered
acutely aware of passing moments
brewing coffee
gathering ghosts;
shuffles to the table in
uncertain dress shoes,
closer to dad in ways
none of us want to notice.
Six months to three years.
Stories flicker behind his milky blindness
stories of a lifetime that
I missed, somehow.
They surface in waves,
paw at the sand, stealing only
so many grains at a time

to put in my pocket
to take home.
Six months to three years.
We chatter, he weeps.
We eat cake and more cake
until words disintegrate in
our sugared mouths.
Until all we want is
the comfort of
breathing the same air.

Uncommon Ritual
(Columbine)

Twinkle twinkle little stars
Heaven's showing off its scars
Fifteen children lie
Sleeping soundly
Sleeping deeply
Sleep forever
Sleep in peace.

One lavender April morning
One bright with streaks of
Yellow crayon sun
Two warm feet hit the floor running
One each:
Favorite pink blouse
Pair of stonewash stretch jeans
Pair of sweat socks
Pair of scuffed white Reeboks
Pair of tiny diamond earrings
Two assignments to complete
Before 2:00 class but
There would be time
There would be time to finish later
And a test to study for tomorrow
But right now a flurry of hair
Barely combed, orange juice and
Chatter, a laugh
Down the stairs and out the door
She's gone.
One April morning.

The other two
Rubbing their faces like stew bums

Up since before dawn
They're yawning
They're counting minutes
Counting bullets
Loading guns
Soaking cotton with liquid propane
And wrapping bombs like gifts
It'll be just like a movie
An explosion just like in a movie
Imagine the smoke
Lots of smoke
We burst in the door with
Light streaming behind us like
A child's crayon sun
Point our guns
Watch 'em run away
Just like in a movie
Make them go away
One each:
Black sweater
Pair of black jeans
Pair of black socks
Pair of scuffed white Reeboks
In a swirl of black trenchcoats
Flapping like Zorro's cape
They're out the door and gone.
One April morning.

Twinkle twinkle little stars
You'll see who your masters are
You'll be sorry then
Sorry you laughed at us

Sorry you whispered behind our backs
That you weren't our friends.

One girl in tears outside the high school
Could barely speak but told the reporter
Explosions started in the library around eleven
There was smoke
Lots of smoke
Two figures in the doorway
Light streamed in behind them
They had guns
It was just like a movie
One laughed
One shot off some rounds
Everyone screamed
Tried to run away
Tried to get away
She couldn't see because of the smoke
Wasn't sure exactly how many
Classmates were killed
In the library.
In the cafeteria
More explosions
One called out names, aimed and fired
Blood spattered on his hands
She crouched behind the Coke machine
They kept shooting
One of them shouted This is awesome
One girl in a pink blouse hiding under a table
Looked up at the gunman aiming at her face
He asked Do you believe in god?
She answered Yes
Before he pulled the trigger.
The crying girl told the reporter

Five of her friends had been hurt:
One Ashley
One Kelly
One Jennifer and
Two Allisons.

Twinkle twinkle little stars
We still wonder who you are
The earth has wounds to heal
It's still bleeding
It's still bleeding
It's still bleeding.

Conversation in Color

We walk beneath an undecided sky,
mom and I, thunderheads creeping like
glaciers into the summer blue; silver
underside of leaves blowing backward.

I watch the way she watches the afternoon
light lose its definition, change shadows to
soft tones of sameness; remember how
we'd argue about blending colors, painting

the strangeness of a day like today when her
thoughts were the opaque certainty of oils
and mine, transparent layers of watercolor.
I open the lawn chair I carry, she rests

helpless arthritic hands in her lap too twisted
now to hold a paintbrush, too hard to control
since the stroke. We start back toward home
into the grey-green scent of rain.

People on The Street Exploding

It happens in those
strange pockets of silence when
the emphysematous city inhales
and fails, for a moment, to expire;
when fast-food wrappers form
a garden border along the curb
and whirling dirt pretends
the serenity of falling snow.
It happens that I hear them,
people on the street exploding
blistered souls peeling away from
their owners, hanging by only one,
perhaps precious, thread
that just snaps.
Step on a crack.
Step on a crack and break somebody's back.
Step on a crack.
Step on a crack and somebody else explodes
free falls, hits the pavement
bursts into verbal flames
about how he lost his job
about how she lost her self-respect
about how we're all lost and Jesus
will save us if we only listen.
It happens that I hear them
shatter like a storefront window
hit with a brick.
Step on a crack.
Step on a crack and privacy rains painful upon us.
Step on a crack.
Step on a crack and frailty crunches under our feet
and someone is buried like a landmine
and someone is trapped like the ocean in a seashell
and someone is consumed like the heart of a star
when it dies.

Gold and Purple

Kindergarten class picture day
the black-and-white nuns
of the Blessed Virgin Mary
assembled us by height
all cherub-like, smiling
in slippery white,
in tin-foil halos
in poster board wings
with lick-n-stick stars
and pasted pastel ribbons.
They pulled me out of place, said
these wings are not right
these wings are too dark
these wings will turn black
in the photograph.

But at home they were
glorious glittering things.
She worked all week
at the dining room table
pressing layer upon layer
of gold and purple sparkles
into the glue with her hands
until all the white was gone.
Now they were not right,
too dark, turning black
and the nuns said take them off
but I couldn't.
I don't know how she attached them,
those damned wings
flapping on my back
in the wind,
walking home.

I See Faces

I see faces in the trees,
twisted features
merged from knurling knots
and twining shadow;
secret creatures
conjured by the unwitting
play of sun across the
surface of wordless furrows;
mysteries stirred from
the depth of earth's memory.
They bare their knuckles to
the anguish of being
silenced,
the failing day
and twilight sleep.
They are not dead, but speak.
They do not live, but witness
these moments
these stories
these dreams.

Morning on Cape Cod

It is quiet here, only the rattle of beach grass
dancing in the Atlantic breeze;
grey waves sketching secrets on the shore.
Pages of my paperback flip randomly,

dancing in the Atlantic breeze.
The language of morning light shimmers;
pages of my paperback flip randomly.
Iridescent patterns upon the sand

the language of morning light shimmers
sings without the weight of words.
Iridescent patterns upon the sand
scripted by what the wind would tell us

sing without the weight of words.
Grey waves sketching secrets on the shore
scripted by what the wind would tell us.
It is quiet here, only the rattle of beach grass.

The Kennedys Are Dead

Hyannisport sure
it's a tourist town;
weekenders saunter up and down
Main Street in summer prints,
awning stripes; point at this
and that, point here
and there, go in
and out
every souvenir shop
stocked with the same
saltwater taffy and fudge
and postcards of
the Kennedys from the fifties.
When life was good.
There they are.
By the cash register.
Jack and Jackie.
Happy.
Like it never happened. And
if you visit St. Francis Xavier
Church on South Water
Sunday mornings you just
might catch a glimpse… but
it's over now, folks.
Go back to your homes,
nothing to see here.
The Kennedys are dead.
Even John-John
revolves on a rack
between a lighthouse
and a lobster.

Waking

a flurry of words
like snow caught in
lashes fluttering for sight
those nights when aware
I can see the limits of
vision from the inside
if I open my eyes
all the words will burn
away in the light
along with sleepless
vapor of dreams that
rise from my skin
fly without form
disappear into the morning

Poems 2006 - 2014

Garden in Autumn

They lose their strength these last few weeks
shriveled, spotted, translucent in the incidental
light of brown October, resigned to display a
different, bony kind of beauty; listen to a
wisdom hidden deep in the root that whispers
your work is complete
your season has passed.
So I, too, must respond to the hardened ground
the dry rattle of autumn and reluctant, tend to
their winter bed, ready them for the cold sleep
ahead and for me, long months of remembering
the stain of green on my fingers
the smell of earth in my hands.

Patterns

white wax drips from the ritual candle, an afterthought of inspiration and holy fire runs a warm path along my thigh and stops, spent, suspended in creation's redundant patterns a comet a raindrop a tadpole a bean sprout a bead of sweat a seed of semen a stream of lava a melting dream the blood on a scalpel a distress signal from the Titanic an unexpected tear a splash of paint from a renegade artist's brush whose rhythm spills a vision beyond the edge of this canvas sheet and forms the negative space between our bodies and the distance of the stars.

Gas

So cold since last night
only the empty radiator
clanking, cars crunching
across the crusted parkway.
We sit inside;
steam floats from your
almost warm morning cup.
You say they say that
helium was created within
the first six seconds of the
universe. I ask how one
calculates the meanness of
the January sun as it ricochets
off the glaze of yesterday's ice
storm; burns without heat through
our unwashed windows; makes
the out-of-focus snow-covered
magnolia appear to be in full bloom.
You say they say that
original helium is not the same
as we know it, the molecular
structure is different and
found only in deep space.
I ask why the chemistry of
far-flung creation's gas
continues to complicate
our conversation.
We sit inside
sipping coffee in the silent
but completely relevant cold.

Walking into Glass

I know what love is. It's a glass door
I keep walking into, the decisive crack
of the pane against my forehead that
leaves me dumbstruck, a fixed target
when shards start to drop hard and
precise as knives, shattering into a
million words I can't understand. It's
wobbling like a drunk on the border
between inside and out, unable to
distinguish one from the other, the
crunch of footsteps on my reflection
sounds the same in either direction. I
know what it is. It's those little pricks of
pain, those tiny invisible splinters of you
that work themselves to the surface,
reminding me of something broken.

Player Dog

Player Dog Rest in Peace
spray-painted on the railroad overpass high
above the expressway. It's part of the drive
an anonymous prayer I read every day
testament to the short life of a kid with
a gang name attached to him like a toe-tag
his case closed before his coffin did.

The Union Pacific bridge is peeling orange crud
and bleeding rust but I can still see what's left of
the death-defying memorial scrawled in the heat
of the closest thing they knew to grief
dangling over the side, a two-story drop to
the traffic, the meaning of the rail's warning:
WILL NOT CLEAR MAN.

Player Dog Rest in Peace
just before I reach my halfway point, where
the speed picks up at Independence Avenue
heading downtown. It's part of the ride
an off ramp to nowhere.
It tells me where I am
and how much farther I have to go.

Cigarette Break

Light one up and out he comes.
You got a smoke?
No.
He comes from nowhere.
He comes too close.
You got a smoke?
No.
You got a light?
No.
You got some change?
No.
He squints at me hard.
Sometimes he spits.
He calls himself the king of the street.

Sometimes I give up
give him a cigarette
pay my dues for the use of his sidewalk.
All I want is a quiet break.

Goddamn raggedy bagman.
He always comes too close.
You got a smoke?
Yeah.
You got a light?
Yeah.
You got some change?
Yeah.
Startling, how simple it is
the twisted etiquette of want
the uneven economy of need
the daily exchange of weakness at
the rate of four syllables to one.

Joyride

That convertible parked at the curb.
That smooth ice-blue coupe with chrome molding
and shark fins sharp enough to slice a strip of
highway into tiny hundred-mile-an-hour shreds.
Just sitting there, tempting me to squeal those
wheels over yesterday's grit, kick up clouds
that swirl like cyclones, fishtail headlong and
hair flying into the curves of summer, radio
blaring and afternoon glare on the windshield
into I-don't-give-a-shit nights where the cool
bright moon shines like a hood ornament, only
a short drive from anywhere. Take me away
take me wherever you want, let me sit in the
passenger seat with no one at the wheel.

Private Ceremony

he stands on a hill somewhere in Scotland
weary of the weight of his own skin
earthbound as stone, he longs for his bride
imagines he hears her voice in the wind

weary of the weight of his own skin
he casts her ashes like sugar to the sky
imagines he hears her voice in the wind
her muddy boots still on the stairs in Chicago

he casts her ashes like sugar to the sky
sees her dancing away on the air
her muddy boots still on the stairs in Chicago
he stands on a hill somewhere in Scotland

Sad as Juliet

Romance is a dance, a pas de deux that
seduces even the clumsiest among us to
pirouette, leap and piqué around until
the violins begin to slip out of tune, we
lose our balance and the graceful ballet
collapses into a pounding chorus line of
synchronized smiles, sweaty lies under
hot lights and predictable repetitions that
kick two three and turn two three into
oh baby baby oh and show me your panties.
You have no choice but to let it die
though through no means so noble as
the quick kill from a happy dagger or
a swill of poisonous potion to make it stop.
No, it's more embarrassing. More like a
cold nipple poking through your costume,
or stumbling as you strut across the stage. But
sadder. Sad as a dropped cue or forgotten line.
Sad as Juliet left hanging, at a loss for words
one night, outside on the balcony.

Higher Ground

We walk toward the river's edge
this morning of the third day to see
if it has risen overnight. To see if
we'll be swept away or kept from
harm on higher ground. We'd lain
awake the night before, felt the
weight of the storm press hard upon
the roof, heard it fling itself sideways
against the windows. When you thought
I was asleep, you went to the basement
to check for flooding and I waited for
you to disappear down the stairs before
I looked for leaks along the ceiling.

Silent as shadows now, you and I in the
early morning, walking to the river
heads bowed like the others who pass
like ghosts through this wall of steadily
falling rain, listening to the sky rumble
like a bellyache above us, above us all
above all our homes.
What can we do?
What can we save?
What will be lost?
We walk until we find the river's answer
swirling round our legs, clinging to our skin
dripping from our useless hands.

Winter Sky

Unusual, such a beautiful afternoon
so late in November. So blindingly bright.
Linear clouds cross the thin winter sky
like trails left by the blades of a skater.
I think of you, so far from reach.

It's hard. Hard to feel anything but cold.
Hard to keep from clawing at heaven, from
ripping its flimsy fabric wide open in hope of
finding you among the music and angels who
joyous, tumble back to earth like snow.

There is no comfort in these childish visions.
No compassion in the shadows of God's
brilliant light. So still is death. I hear nothing
but restless leaves rattle across frozen grass.
Nothing, save the sound of my own breath.

Spring Rain (Poetry Month)

Poets roam the cobblestones in search of
rhymes or reason it is the season when
rain falls sideways and tulips burst into flame
when word and image run away laughing
like the dish and the spoon and the
lost art of lunacy returns in full bloom
when the Muse lifts her threadbare skirt
and splashes like a child through diamond
puddles left between the verses of an April storm
dances dances dances until stones turn soft
beneath her feet, blur like ink on wrinkled paper.

Late Bloomer

Here, take this winter skin.
Wrap it around your bones.
Tight. Tighter, to keep out the cold.
To cover what's exposed, to protect
the precious mechanics of becoming
something beautiful. You poke out
at every angle like a little twig
swallowed by the snow,
holding tight to those stubborn buds
that refused to burst in summer
when it would've been
too simple a task, too expected,
and much less appreciated.

www.ingramcontent.com/pod-product-compliance
Lightning Source LLC
Chambersburg PA
CBHW042345300426
44110CB00030B/172